Susanna Tee

Cupcakes

This edition published in 2011

LOVE FOOD is an imprint of Parragon Books Ltd

Parragon

Queen Street House

4 Queen Street

Bath BA1 1HE, UK

ISBN: 978-1-4075-0364-6

Printed in China

Created and produced by the Bridgewater Book Company Ltd

Photographer: Laurie Evans

Home economist: Fergal Connolly

Notes for the Reader

This book uses metric and imperial measurements. Follow the same units of measurement
throughout; do not mix metric and imperial . All spoon measurements are level: teaspoons are
assumed to be 5 ml, and tablespoons are assumed to be 15 ml. Unless otherwise stated, milk is
assumed to be whole, eggs and individual vegetables such as potatoes are medium, and pepper is
freshly ground black pepper. Recipes using raw or very lightly cooked eggs
should be avoided by infants, the elderly, pregnant women, convalescents,
and anyone suffering from an illness.

contents

introduction

Who can resist a cupcake, and what is it that makes them so appealing? Why are they loved by children and adults alike? Perhaps it is their size that makes them so tempting — after all, you can have an individual, diminutive cake all to yourself!

A children's party isn't complete without a batch of sticky, iced cupcakes. Cupcakes are often called fairy cakes, and they are in fact one and the same thing, but we tend to think of a plain cake mixture, topped with an icing, as a fairy cake, and a more elaborate cake mixture as a cupcake.

There are several theories on the origin of cupcakes, and they probably all have some truth in them. Some people believe that, as these little cakes were originally baked in cups, which is evident in some old cookbooks, this is how they came to be called cupcakes. Other people believe that the name may have come from the amount of the basic ingredients used to make a cake, with the addition of eggs and any flavourings. In

Britain, for example, old recipes called for a cupful of sugar, a cupful of butter and a cupful of flour. In America, meanwhile, the measuring system is actually based on cupfuls of ingredients. Nowadays, in both America and Britain, the term 'cupcake' is used for a small cake baked in a fluted paper baking case, a cup or a cup-shaped mould.

Fluted paper baking cases retain the cakes, and help to keep them moist and fresh for longer. The usual sizes for cases are mini, measuring 3 cm/1¼ inches; standard, measuring 4.5 cm/1¾ inches; and large (muffin), measuring 5.5 cm/2¼ inches. They are also available in various colours, the most usual being white or brown, but they are also available in silver, gold, and printed with a decoration. There are even reusable baking cases available, which are made of silicone and are brightly coloured. Cupcakes can also be made in flexible ovenware cupcake moulds, but these are used without the paper cases and obviously the resulting cupcakes do not look quite the same.

Also look out for different decorations. There are a wide variety of these too, from small, silver balls and various chocolates, to crystallized flowers and elaborate chocolate flowers.

Cupcakes are quick and easy to make and some of the recipes in this book are made by the all-in-one method, where all the ingredients are put in one bowl and beaten together for even quicker results. Many of the recipes suggest using soft tub margarine but, since there is such a bewildering array of margarines on the market, make sure you choose a soft tub margarine that is labelled 'suitable for baking'. These are ideal for whipping up a batch of cupcakes in no time at all. However, for flavour and a natural product, you cannot do better than using butter. If it is rock hard when you want to use it, pop it in the microwave on a high setting for 10 seconds to soften slightly.

If you need a basic recipe to create your own cupcakes, a cake mixture made with 115 g/4 oz butter, 115 g/4 oz sugar, 115 g/4 oz flour and 2 eggs makes about 12 standard-sized cupcakes. To make a basic chocolate cupcake mixture, replace 1 tablespoon of the flour with 1 tablespoon of cocoa powder. Fill the paper cases about two-thirds full and bake in an oven preheated to 180°C/350°F/Gas Mark 4 for about 20 minutes. A butter cream icing made with 85 g/3 oz butter and 175 g/6 oz icing sugar, or glacé icing made with 175 g/ 6 oz icing sugar and 2–3 teaspoons of water, is sufficient to top them.

In this book, you are spoilt for choice. There are Family Favourites, such as Sticky Gingerbread Cupcakes; Fruit Cupcakes, all bursting with fruit, such as moist Apple Streusel Cupcakes; and Chocolate Sensations, a chapter of chocolate cupcakes all to themselves! Finally there are Festive Creations for all occasions, from Christmas Cupcakes to The Cupcake Wedding Cake. These are irresistible cakes worthy of any occasion, whether afternoon tea, a supper party, a classroom birthday, a cake sale or even a wedding. Why not get baking right away?

family favourites

Although these are perhaps the simplest of cupcakes, they have been popular since the eighteenth century. In those days they were baked in individual fluted tins and not in paper cases as they are today.

queen cakes

Makes 18 cupcakes

115 g/4 oz butter, softened,
    or soft tub margarine

115 g/4 oz caster sugar

2 large eggs, lightly beaten

4 tsp lemon juice

175 g/6 oz self-raising white flour

115 g/4 oz currants

2–4 tbsp milk, if necessary

★ Preheat the oven to 190°C/375°F/Gas Mark 5. Put 18 paper baking cases in a bun tray, or 18 double-layer paper cases on a baking tray.

★ Put the butter and sugar in a bowl and beat together until light and fluffy. Gradually beat in the eggs, then beat in the lemon juice with 1 tablespoon of the flour. Using a metal spoon, fold in the remaining flour and the currants, adding a little milk, if necessary, to give a soft dropping consistency. Spoon the mixture into the paper cases.

★ Bake the cupcakes in the preheated oven for 15–20 minutes, or until well risen and golden brown. Transfer to a wire rack and leave to cool.

These honey-soaked cupcakes are inspired by the Greek spiced honey cakes known as 'Melomakárona'. They are for all those with a sweet tooth and, of course, lovers of honey!

drizzled honey cupcakes

Makes 12 cupcakes

85 g/3 oz self-raising white flour

1/4 tsp ground cinnamon

pinch of ground cloves

pinch of grated nutmeg

85 g/3 oz butter, softened

85 g/3 oz caster sugar

1 tbsp clear honey

finely grated rind of 1 orange

2 eggs, lightly beaten

40 g/1 1/2 oz walnut pieces, finely chopped

Topping

15 g/1/2 oz walnut pieces, finely chopped

1/4 tsp ground cinnamon

2 tbsp clear honey

juice of 1 orange

★ Preheat the oven to 190°C/375°F/Gas Mark 5. Put 12 paper baking cases in a bun tray, or put 12 double-layer paper cases on a baking tray.

★ Sift the flour, cinnamon, cloves and nutmeg together into a bowl. Put the butter and sugar in a separate bowl and beat together until light and fluffy. Beat in the honey and orange rind, then gradually add the eggs, beating well after each addition. Using a metal spoon, fold in the flour mixture. Stir in the walnuts, then spoon the mixture into the paper cases.

★ Bake the cupcakes in the preheated oven for 20 minutes, or until well risen and golden brown. Transfer to a wire rack and leave to cool.

★ To make the topping, mix together the walnuts and cinnamon. Put the honey and orange juice in a saucepan and heat gently, stirring, until combined.

★ When the cupcakes have almost cooled, prick the tops all over with a fork or skewer and then drizzle with the warm honey mixture. Sprinkle the walnut mixture over the top of each cupcake and serve warm or cold.

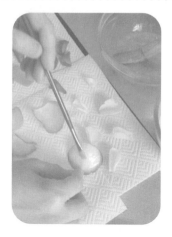

Rose essence might seem like an unusual ingredient, but it gives a subtle floral flavour to these little cakes.

rose petal cupcakes

Makes 12 cupcakes

115 g/4 oz butter, softened

115 g/4 oz caster sugar

2 eggs, lightly beaten

1 tbsp milk

few drops of essence of rose oil

$^1/_4$ tsp vanilla extract

175 g/6 oz self-raising white flour

silver dragées (cake decoration
    balls), to decorate

Icing

85 g/3 oz butter, softened

175 g/6 oz icing sugar

pink or purple food colouring
    (optional)

Crystallized rose petals

12–24 rose petals

lightly beaten egg white, for
    brushing

caster sugar, for sprinkling

★ To make the crystallized rose petals, gently rinse the petals and dry well with kitchen paper. Using a pastry brush, paint both sides of a rose petal with egg white, then coat well with caster sugar. Place on a tray and repeat with the remaining petals. Cover the tray with kitchen foil and leave to dry overnight.

★ Preheat the oven to 200°C/400°F/Gas Mark 6. Put 12 paper baking cases in a bun tray, or put 12 double-layer paper cases on a baking tray.

★ Put the butter and sugar in a bowl and beat together until light and fluffy. Gradually add the eggs, beating well after each addition. Stir in the milk, rose essence and vanilla extract then, using a metal spoon, fold in the flour. Spoon the mixture into the paper cases.

★ Bake the cupcakes in the preheated oven for 12–15 minutes, or until well risen and golden brown. Transfer to a wire rack and leave to cool.

★ To make the icing, put the butter in a large bowl and beat until fluffy. Sift in the icing sugar and mix well together. If wished, add a few drops of pink or purple food colouring to complement the rose petals.

★ When the cupcakes are cold, spread the icing on top of each cake. Top with 1–2 crystallized rose petals and sprinkle with silver dragées to decorate.

Unlike many cupcakes, these family favourites will keep for several days in an airtight tin because they are rich, sticky and moist — if you can resist eating them, that is!

sticky gingerbread cupcakes

Makes 16 cupcakes

115 g/4 oz plain white flour

2 tsp ground ginger

³/₄ tsp ground cinnamon

I piece of stem ginger, finely chopped

³/₄ tsp bicarbonate of soda

4 tbsp milk

85 g/3 oz butter, softened, or soft tub margarine

70 g/2¹/₂ oz soft dark brown sugar

2 tbsp black treacle

2 eggs, lightly beaten

I piece of stem ginger, to decorate

Icing

85 g/3 oz butter, softened

175/6 oz icing sugar

2 tbsp ginger syrup from the stem ginger jar

★ Preheat the oven to 160°C/325°F/Gas Mark 3. Put 16 paper baking cases in a bun tray, or place 16 double-layer paper cases on a baking tray.

★ Sift the flour, ground ginger and cinnamon together into a bowl. Add the chopped ginger and toss in the flour mixture until well coated. In a separate bowl, dissolve the bicarbonate of soda in the milk.

★ Put the butter and sugar in a bowl and beat together until fluffy. Beat in the treacle, then gradually add the eggs, beating well after each addition. Beat in the flour mixture, then gradually beat in the milk. Spoon the mixture into the paper cases.

★ Bake the cupcakes in the preheated oven for 20 minutes, or until well risen and golden brown. Transfer to a wire rack and leave to cool.

★ To make the icing, put the butter in a bowl and beat until fluffy. Sift in the icing sugar, add the ginger syrup and beat together until smooth and creamy. Slice the stem ginger into thin slivers or chop finely.

★ When the cupcakes are cold, spread the icing on top of each cupcake, then decorate with pieces of the ginger.

These little cakes are always a favourite with children, but who can resist them when baked in large muffin cases, topped with a swirl of creamy frosting?

frosted peanut butter cupcakes

Makes 16 cupcakes

55 g/2 oz butter, softened, or soft
    tub margarine
225 g/8 oz soft light brown sugar
115 g/4 oz crunchy peanut butter
2 eggs, lightly beaten
I tsp vanilla extract
225 g/8 oz plain white flour
2 tsp baking powder
100 ml/3½ fl oz milk
Frosting
200 g/7 oz full-fat soft cream cheese
25 g/I oz butter, softened
225 g/8 oz icing sugar

★ Preheat the oven to 180°C/350°F/Gas Mark 4. Put 16 muffin paper cases in muffin trays.

★ Put the butter, sugar and peanut butter in a bowl and beat together for 1–2 minutes, or until well mixed. Gradually add the eggs, beating well after each addition, then add the vanilla extract. Sift in the flour and baking powder and then, using a metal spoon, fold them into the mixture, alternating with the milk. Spoon the mixture into the paper cases.

★ Bake the cupcakes in the preheated oven for 25 minutes, or until well risen and golden brown. Transfer to a wire rack and leave to cool.

★ To make the frosting, put the cream cheese and butter in a large bowl and, using an electric hand whisk, beat together until smooth. Sift the icing sugar into the mixture, then beat together until well mixed.

★ When the cupcakes are cold, spread the frosting on top of each cupcake, swirling it with a round-bladed knife. Store the cupcakes in the refrigerator until ready to serve.

Almonds are often the first choice of nut when making cakes but in Italy, where they are in plentiful supply, walnuts are often used. They give the cupcakes a moist texture as well as a delicious flavour.

moist walnut cupcakes

Makes 12 cupcakes

85 g/3 oz walnuts

55 g/2 oz butter, softened

100 g/3½ oz caster sugar

grated rind of ½ lemon

70 g/2½ oz self-raising white flour

2 eggs

12 walnut halves, to decorate

Icing

55 g/2 oz butter, softened

85 g/3 oz icing sugar

grated rind of ½ lemon

1 tsp lemon juice

★ Preheat the oven to 190°C/375°F/Gas Mark 5. Put 12 paper baking cases in a bun tray, or put 12 double-layer paper cases on a baking tray.

★ Put the walnuts in a food processor and, using a pulsating action, blend until finely ground, being careful not to over-grind, which will turn them to oil. Add the butter, cut into small pieces, along with the sugar, lemon rind, flour and eggs, then blend until evenly mixed. Spoon the mixture into the paper cases.

★ Bake the cupcakes in the preheated oven for 20 minutes, or until well risen and golden brown. Transfer to a wire rack and leave to cool.

★ To make the icing, put the butter in a bowl and beat until fluffy. Sift in the icing sugar, add the lemon rind and juice and mix well together.

★ When the cupcakes are cold, spread the icing on top of each cupcake and top with a walnut half to decorate.

If you haven't feather-iced a cake before, you will be surprised how easy it is to do, and the result is very effective.

feather-iced coffee cupcakes

Makes 16 cupcakes

1 tbsp instant coffee granules

1 tbsp boiling water

115 g/4 oz butter, softened, or soft tub margarine

115 g/4 oz soft light brown sugar

2 eggs

115 g/4 oz self-raising white flour

1/2 tsp baking powder

2 tbsp soured cream

Icing

225 g/8 oz icing sugar

4 tsp warm water

1 tsp instant coffee granules

2 tsp boiling water

★ Preheat the oven to 190°C/375°F/Gas Mark 5. Put 16 paper baking cases in a bun tray, or put 16 double-layer paper cases on a baking tray.

★ Put the coffee granules in a cup or small bowl, add the boiling water and stir until dissolved. Leave to cool slightly.

★ Put the butter, sugar and eggs in a bowl. Sift in the flour and baking powder, then beat the ingredients together until smooth. Add the dissolved coffee and the soured cream and beat together until well mixed. Spoon the mixture into the paper cases.

★ Bake the cupcakes in the preheated oven for 20 minutes, or until well risen and golden brown. Transfer to a wire rack and leave to cool.

★ To make the icing, sift 85 g/3 oz of the icing sugar into a bowl, then gradually mix in the warm water to make a coating consistency that will cover the back of a wooden spoon. Dissolve the coffee granules in the boiling water. Sift the remaining icing sugar into a bowl, then stir in the dissolved coffee granules. Spoon the icing into a piping bag fitted with a piping nozzle. When the cupcakes are cold, coat the tops with the white icing, then quickly pipe the coffee icing in parallel lines on top. Using a skewer, draw it across the piped lines in both directions. Leave to set before serving.

fruit cupcakes

fruit cupcakes

Coconut and glacé cherries make these little cakes really moist, and give them a sweet flavour that will make them a hit with children.

coconut cherry cakes

Makes 12 cupcakes

115 g/4 oz butter, softened, or soft tub margarine

115 g/4 oz caster sugar

2 tbsp milk

2 eggs, lightly beaten

85 g/3 oz self-raising white flour

1/2 tsp baking powder

85 g/3 oz desiccated coconut

115 g/4 oz glacé cherries, quartered

8 whole glacé, maraschino or fresh cherries, to decorate

Icing

55 g/2 oz butter, softened

115 g/4 oz icing sugar

1 tbsp milk

★ Preheat the oven to 180°C/350°F/Gas Mark 4. Put 12 paper baking cases in a bun tray, or put 12 double-layer paper cases on a baking tray.

★ Put the butter and sugar in a bowl and beat together until light and fluffy. Stir in the milk. Gradually add the eggs, beating well after each addition. Sift in the flour and baking powder and fold them in with the coconut. Gently fold in most of the quartered cherries. Spoon the mixture into the paper cases and scatter the remaining quartered cherries on top.

★ Bake the cupcakes in the preheated oven for 20–25 minutes, or until well risen, golden brown and firm to the touch. Transfer to a wire rack and leave to cool.

★ To make the butter cream icing, put the butter in a bowl and beat until fluffy. Sift in the icing sugar and beat together until well mixed, gradually beating in the milk.

★ To decorate the cupcakes, using a piping bag fitted with a large star nozzle, pipe the butter cream on top of each cupcake, then add a glacé, maraschino or fresh cherry to decorate.

These are large cupcakes because they are baked in muffin cases —
for this delicious recipe, a small cupcake simply wouldn't be enough!

carrot & orange cupcakes with mascarpone icing

Makes 12 cupcakes

115 g/4 oz butter, softened, or soft tub margarine

115 g/4 oz soft light brown sugar

juice and finely grated rind of 1 small orange

2 large eggs, lightly beaten

175 g/6 oz carrots, grated

25 g/1 oz walnut pieces, roughly chopped

125 g/4½ oz plain white flour

1 tsp ground mixed spice

1½ tsp baking powder

Icing

280 g/10 oz mascarpone cheese

4 tbsp icing sugar

grated rind of 1 large orange

★ Preheat the oven to 180°C/350°F/Gas Mark 4. Put 12 muffin paper cases in a muffin tray.

★ Put the butter, sugar and orange rind in a bowl and beat together until light and fluffy. Gradually add the eggs, beating well after each addition. Squeeze any excess liquid from the carrots and add to the mixture with the walnuts and orange juice. Stir into the mixture until well mixed. Sift in the flour, mixed spice and baking powder and then, using a metal spoon, fold into the mixture. Spoon the mixture into the paper cases.

★ Bake the cupcakes in the preheated oven for 25 minutes, or until well risen, firm to the touch and golden brown. Transfer to a wire rack and leave to cool.

★ To make the icing, put the mascarpone cheese, icing sugar and orange **rind** in a large bowl and beat together until well mixed.

★ When the cupcakes are cold, spread the icing on top of each cupcake, swirling it with a round-bladed knife. Store the cupcakes in the refrigerator until ready to serve.

Butterfly cakes may remind you of children's birthday parties, but these attractive, creamy, miniature delights are popular with adults too.

lemon butterfly cakes

Makes 12 cupcakes

115 g/4 oz self-raising white flour

½ tsp baking powder

115 g/4 oz soft tub margarine

115 g/4 oz caster sugar

2 eggs, lightly beaten

finely grated rind of ½ lemon

2 tbsp milk

icing sugar, for dusting

Lemon filling

85 g/3 oz butter, softened

175/6 oz icing sugar

1 tbsp lemon juice

★ Preheat the oven to 190°C/375°F/Gas Mark 5. Put 12 paper baking cases in a bun tray, or put 12 double-layer paper cases on a baking tray.

★ Sift the flour and baking powder into a large bowl. Add the margarine, sugar, eggs, lemon rind and milk and, using an electric hand whisk, beat together until smooth. Spoon the mixture into the paper cases.

★ Bake the cupcakes in the preheated oven for 15–20 minutes, or until well risen and golden brown. Transfer to a wire rack and leave to cool.

★ To make the filling, put the butter in a bowl and beat until fluffy. Sift in the icing sugar, add the lemon juice and beat together until smooth and creamy.

★ When the cupcakes are cold, use a serrated knife to cut a circle from the top of each cupcake and then cut each circle in half. Spread or pipe a little of the butter cream filling into the centre of each cupcake, then press 2 semi-circular halves into it at an angle to resemble butterfly wings. Dust with sifted icing sugar before serving.

These cupcakes are another children's favourite, but the addition of pecan nuts gives them a little sophistication, in case you needed an excuse to try them!

banana & pecan cupcakes

Makes 24 cupcakes

225 g/8 oz plain white flour

1¼ tsp baking powder

¼ tsp bicarbonate of soda

2 ripe bananas

115 g/4 oz butter, softened, or soft tub margarine

115 g/4 oz caster sugar

½ tsp vanilla extract

2 eggs, lightly beaten

4 tbsp soured cream

55 g/2 oz pecan nuts, roughly chopped

Topping

115 g/4 oz butter, softened

115 g/4 oz icing sugar

25 g/1 oz pecan nuts, finely chopped

★ Preheat the oven to 190°C/375°F/Gas Mark 5. Put 24 paper baking cases in a bun tray, or put 24 double-layer paper cases on a baking tray.

★ Sift together the flour, baking powder and bicarbonate of soda. Peel the bananas, put them in a bowl and mash with a fork.

★ Put the butter, sugar and vanilla in a bowl and beat together until light and fluffy. Gradually add the eggs, beating well after each addition. Stir in the mashed bananas and soured cream. Using a metal spoon, fold in the sifted flour mixture and chopped nuts, then spoon the mixture into the paper cases.

★ Bake the cupcakes in the preheated oven for 20 minutes, or until well risen and golden brown. Transfer to a wire rack and leave to cool.

★ To make the topping, put the butter in a bowl and beat until fluffy. Sift in the icing sugar and mix together well. Spread the icing on top of each cupcake and sprinkle with the finely chopped pecans before serving.

The tartness of the cranberries contrasts really well with the sweetness of these little cakes.

cranberry cupcakes

Makes 14 cupcakes

75 g/2³/4 oz butter, softened, or soft
   tub margarine

100 g/3¹/2 oz caster sugar

1 large egg

2 tbsp milk

100 g/3¹/2 oz self-raising flour

1 tsp baking powder

75 g/2³/4 oz cranberries, frozen

★ Preheat the oven to 180°C/350°F/Gas Mark 4. Put 14 paper baking cases in a bun tray, or put 14 double-layer paper cases on a baking tray.

★ Put the butter and sugar in a bowl and beat together until light and fluffy. Gradually beat in the egg, then stir in the milk. Sift in the flour and baking powder and, using a large metal spoon, fold them into the mixture. Gently fold in the frozen cranberries. Spoon the mixture into the paper cases.

★ Bake the cupcakes in the preheated oven for 15–20 minutes, or until well risen and golden brown. Transfer to a wire rack and leave to cool.

These soft, subtly spiced apple cupcakes, topped with a buttery streusel layer, really are very moreish. They are best served warm, if possible.

apple streusel cupcakes

Makes 14 cupcakes

½ tsp bicarbonate of soda

280-g/10-oz jar Bramley apple sauce

55 g/2 oz butter, softened, or soft tub margarine

85 g/3 oz demerara sugar

1 large egg, lightly beaten

175 g/6 oz self-raising white flour

½ tsp ground cinnamon

½ tsp freshly ground nutmeg

Topping

50 g/1¾ oz plain white flour

50 g/1¾ oz demerara sugar

¼ tsp ground cinnamon

¼ tsp freshly grated nutmeg

35 g/1¼ oz butter

★ Preheat the oven to 180°C/350°F/Gas Mark 4. Put 14 paper baking cases in a bun tray, or put 14 double-layer paper cases on a baking tray.

★ First make the topping. Put the flour, sugar, cinnamon and nutmeg in a bowl or in the bowl of a food processor. Cut the butter into small pieces, then either rub it in by hand or blend in the processor until the mixture resembles fine breadcrumbs. Set aside while you make the cakes.

★ To make the cupcakes, add the bicarbonate of soda to the jar of Bramley apple sauce and stir until dissolved. Put the butter and sugar in a bowl and beat together until light and fluffy. Gradually beat in the egg. Sift in the flour, cinnamon and nutmeg and, using a large metal spoon, fold into the mixture, alternating with the apple sauce.

★ Spoon the mixture into the paper cases. Scatter the topping over each cupcake to cover the tops and press down gently.

★ Bake the cupcakes in the preheated oven for 20 minutes, or until well risen and golden brown. Leave the cakes for 2–3 minutes before serving warm or transfer to a wire rack and leave to cool.

This recipe shows the true meaning of cupcakes because, as the title suggests, they are baked in a teacup. This also makes them ideal to serve as individual desserts.

warm strawberry cupcakes baked in a teacup

Makes 6 cupcakes

115 g/4 oz butter, softened, plus extra for greasing

4 tbsp strawberry conserve

115 g/4 oz caster sugar

2 eggs, lightly beaten

I tsp vanilla extract

115 g/4 oz self-raising white flour

450 g/I lb small whole fresh strawberries

icing sugar, for dusting

★ Preheat the oven to 180°C/350°F/Gas Mark 4. Grease six 200-ml/7-fl oz heavy round teacups with butter. Spoon 2 teaspoons of the strawberry conserve into the bottom of each teacup.

★ Put the butter and sugar in a bowl and beat together until light and fluffy. Gradually add the eggs, beating well after each addition, then add the vanilla extract. Sift in the flour and, using a large metal spoon, fold it into the mixture. Spoon the mixture into the teacups.

★ Stand the cups in a roasting tin, then pour in enough hot water to come one-third up the sides of the cups. Bake the cupcakes in the preheated oven for 40 minutes, or until well risen and golden brown, and a skewer, inserted in the centre, comes out clean. If over-browning, cover the cupcakes with a sheet of foil. Leave the cupcakes to cool for 2–3 minutes, then carefully lift the cups from the tin and place them on saucers.

★ Scatter a few of the whole strawberries over the cakes, then dust them with sifted icing sugar. Serve warm with the remaining strawberries.

Pineapple, flavoured with lemon or lime, imbues these cupcakes with a taste of the tropics. For maximum effect, serve them for afternoon tea when the sun is shining.

tropical pineapple cupcakes with citrus cream frosting

Makes 12 cupcakes

2 slices of canned pineapple in natural juice

85 g/3 oz butter, softened, or soft tub margarine

85 g/3 oz caster sugar

1 large egg, lightly beaten

85 g/3 oz self-raising white flour

1 tbsp juice from the canned pineapple

Frosting

25 g/1 oz butter, softened

100 g/3½ oz soft cream cheese

grated rind of 1 lemon or lime

100 g/3½ oz icing sugar

1 tsp lemon juice or lime juice

★ Preheat the oven to 180°C/350°F/Gas Mark 4. Put 12 paper baking cases in a bun tray, or put 12 double-layer paper cases on a baking tray.

★ Finely chop the pineapple slices. Put the butter and sugar in a bowl and beat together until light and fluffy. Gradually beat in the egg. Add the flour and, using a large metal spoon, fold into the mixture. Fold in the chopped pineapple and the pineapple juice. Spoon the mixture into the paper cases.

★ Bake the cupcakes in the preheated oven for 20 minutes, or until well risen and golden brown. Transfer to a wire rack and leave to cool.

★ To make the frosting, put the butter and cream cheese in a large bowl and, using an electric hand whisk, beat together until smooth. Add the rind from the lemon or lime. Sift the icing sugar into the mixture, then beat together until well mixed. Gradually beat in the juice from the lemon or lime, adding enough to form a spreading consistency.

★ When the cupcakes are cold, spread the frosting on top of each cake, or fill a piping bag fitted with a large star nozzle and pipe the frosting on top. Store the cupcakes in the refrigerator until ready to serve.

Moist with the addition of almonds and flavoured with orange, these cupcakes have a final topping of shredded orange rind in syrup, which increases their moistness and enhances their prettiness.

shredded orange cupcakes

Makes 12 cupcakes

85 g/3 oz butter, softened, or soft tub margarine

85 g/3 oz caster sugar

1 large egg, lightly beaten

85 g/3 oz self-raising white flour

25 g/1 oz ground almonds

grated rind and juice of 1 small orange

Orange topping

1 orange

55 g/2 oz caster sugar

15 g/½ oz toasted flaked almonds

★ Preheat the oven to 180°C/350°F/Gas Mark 4. Put 12 paper baking cases in a bun tray, or put 12 double-layer paper cases on a baking tray.

★ Put the butter and sugar in a bowl and beat together until light and fluffy. Gradually beat in the egg. Add the flour, ground almonds and orange rind and, using a large metal spoon, fold into the mixture. Fold in the orange juice. Spoon the mixture into the paper cases.

★ Bake the cupcakes in the preheated oven for 20–25 minutes, or until well risen and golden brown.

★ Meanwhile, make the topping. Using a citrus zester, pare the rind from the orange, then squeeze the juice. Put the rind, juice and sugar in a saucepan and heat gently, stirring, until the sugar has dissolved, then simmer for 5 minutes.

★ When the cupcakes have cooked, prick them all over with a skewer. Spoon the warm syrup and rind over each cupcake, then scatter the flaked almonds on top. Transfer to a wire rack and leave to cool.

42 42

42 *chocolate sensations*

chocolate sensations

Filled with chocolate butter cream, these appealing little cakes are an all-time favourite with both adults and children.

chocolate butterfly cakes

Makes 12 cupcakes

125 g/4½ oz soft tub margarine

125 g/4½ oz caster sugar

150 g/5½ oz self-raising white flour

2 large eggs

2 tbsp cocoa powder

25 g/1 oz plain chocolate, melted

icing sugar, for dusting

Filling

85 g/3 oz butter, softened

175 g/6 oz icing sugar

25 g/1 oz plain chocolate, melted

★ Preheat the oven to 180°C/350°F/Gas Mark 4. Put 12 paper baking cases in a bun tray, or put 12 double-layer paper cases on a baking tray.

★ Put the margarine, sugar, flour, eggs and cocoa powder in a large bowl and, using an electric hand whisk, beat together until just smooth. Beat in the melted chocolate. Spoon the mixture into the paper cases, filling them three-quarters full.

★ Bake the cupcakes in the preheated oven for 15 minutes, or until springy to the touch. Transfer to a wire rack and leave to cool.

★ To make the filling, put the butter in a bowl and beat until fluffy. Sift in the icing sugar and beat together until smooth. Add the melted chocolate and beat together until well mixed.

★ When the cupcakes are cold, use a serrated knife to cut a circle from the top of each cake and then cut each circle in half. Spread or pipe a little of the butter cream into the centre of each cupcake and press 2 semi-circular halves into it at an angle to resemble butterfly wings. Dust with sifted icing sugar before serving.

A variation on an old favourite, these delicious little cakes will appeal to both children and grown-ups. Leave the cupcakes to chill before serving.

chocolate cupcakes with cream cheese icing

Makes 18 cupcakes

85 g/3 oz butter, softened, or soft tub margarine

100 g/3½ oz caster sugar

2 eggs, lightly beaten

2 tbsp milk

55 g/2 oz plain chocolate chips

225 g/8 oz self-raising white flour

25 g/1 oz cocoa powder

Icing

225 g/8 oz white chocolate

150 g/5½ oz low-fat cream cheese

★ Preheat the oven to 200°C/400°F/Gas Mark 6. Put 18 paper baking cases in 2 bun trays, or put 18 double-layer paper cases on a baking tray.

★ Put the butter and sugar in a bowl and beat together until light and fluffy. Gradually add the eggs, beating well after each addition. Add the milk, then fold in the chocolate chips. Sift in the flour and cocoa powder, then fold into the mixture. Spoon the mixture into the paper cases and smooth the tops.

★ Bake the cupcakes in the preheated oven for 20 minutes, or until well risen and springy to the touch. Transfer to a wire rack and leave to cool.

★ To make the icing, break the chocolate into a small heatproof bowl and set the bowl over a saucepan of gently simmering water until melted. Leave to cool slightly. Put the cream cheese in a bowl and beat until softened, then beat in the slightly cooled chocolate.

★ Spread a little of the icing over the top of each cupcake, then leave to chill in the refrigerator for 1 hour before serving.

These little, light and moist cupcakes, with a tempting fudgy chocolate topping, are perfect for serving at any time of day.

dark & white fudge cupcakes

Makes 20 cupcakes

200 ml/7fl oz water

85 g/3 oz butter

85 g/3 oz caster sugar

1 tbsp golden syrup

3 tbsp milk

1 tsp vanilla extract

1 tsp bicarbonate of soda

225 g/8 oz plain white flour

2 tbsp cocoa powder

Topping

50 g/1³/4 oz plain chocolate

4 tbsp water

50 g/1³/4 oz butter

50 g/1³/4 oz white chocolate

350 g/12 oz icing sugar

Chocolate curls

100 g/3¹/2 oz plain chocolate

100 g/3¹/2 oz white chocolate

★ Preheat the oven to 180°C/350°F/Gas Mark 4. Put 20 paper baking cases in 2 bun trays, or put 20 double-layer paper cases on 2 baking trays.

★ Put the water, butter, sugar and syrup in a saucepan. Heat gently, stirring, until the sugar has dissolved, then bring to the boil. Reduce the heat and cook gently for 5 minutes. Remove from the heat and leave to cool.

★ Meanwhile, put the milk and vanilla extract in a bowl. Add the bicarbonate of soda and stir to dissolve. Sift the flour and cocoa powder into a separate bowl and add the syrup mixture. Stir in the milk and beat until smooth. Spoon the mixture into the paper cases until they are two-thirds full.

★ Bake the cupcakes in the preheated oven for 20 minutes, or until well risen and firm to the touch. Transfer to a wire rack and leave to cool.

★ To make the topping, break the plain chocolate into a small heatproof bowl, add half the water and half the butter, and set the bowl over a saucepan of gently simmering water until melted. Stir until smooth and leave to stand over the water. Repeat with the white chocolate and remaining water and butter. Sift half the icing sugar into each bowl and beat until smooth and thick. Top up the cupcakes with the icings. Leave to set. Serve decorated with chocolate curls made by shaving the chocolate with a potato peeler.

These cupcakes, bursting with chocolate chips, are always irresistible to children so, by baking them in muffin cases, these large varieties should be especially satisfying.

jumbo chocolate chip cupcakes

Makes 8 cupcakes

100 g/3¹/₂ oz soft tub margarine

100 g/3¹/₂ oz caster sugar

2 large eggs

100 g/3¹/₂ oz self-raising white flour

100 g/3¹/₂ oz plain chocolate chips

★ Preheat the oven to 190°C/375°F/Gas Mark 5. Put 8 muffin paper cases in a muffin tray.

★ Put the margarine, sugar, eggs and flour in a large bowl and, using an electric hand whisk, beat together until just smooth. Fold in the chocolate chips. Spoon the mixture into the paper cases.

★ Bake the cupcakes in the preheated oven for 20–25 minutes, or until well risen and golden brown. Transfer to a wire rack to cool.

There is always something fascinating about the appearance of marbled cakes and it is from their appearance that they get their name. When they are cut or bitten into, each slice or bite shows a marble-like swirling of light and dark.

marbled chocolate cupcakes

Makes 21 cupcakes

175 g/6 oz soft tub margarine

175 g/6 oz caster sugar

3 eggs

175 g/6 oz self-raising white flour

2 tbsp milk

55 g/2 oz plain chocolate, melted

★ Preheat the oven to 180°C/350°F/Gas Mark 4. Put 21 paper baking cases in a bun tray, or put 21 double-layer paper cases on a baking tray.

★ Put the margarine, sugar, eggs, flour and milk in a large bowl and, using an electric hand whisk, beat together until just smooth.

★ Divide the mixture between 2 bowls. Add the melted chocolate to one bowl and stir together until well mixed. Using a teaspoon, and alternating the chocolate mixture with the plain mixture, put four half-teaspoons into each paper case.

★ Bake the cupcakes in the preheated oven for 20 minutes, or until well risen and springy to the touch. Transfer to a wire rack and leave to cool.

chocolate sensations

Chocolate chunks packed inside a cupcake produce an irresistible molten-chocolate centre, and they are served warm so that the chocolate really does melt in your mouth.

warm molten-centred chocolate cupcakes

Makes 8 cupcakes

55 g/2 oz soft tub margarine
55 g/2 oz caster sugar
1 large egg
85 g/3 oz self-raising flour
1 tbsp cocoa powder
55 g/2 oz plain chocolate
icing sugar, for dusting

★ Preheat the oven to 190°C/375°F/Gas Mark 5. Put 8 paper baking cases in a bun tray, or put 8 double-layer paper cases on a baking tray.

★ Put the margarine, sugar, egg, flour and cocoa powder in a large bowl and, using an electric hand whisk, beat together until just smooth.

★ Spoon half of the mixture into the paper cases. Using a teaspoon, make an indentation in the centre of each cake. Break the chocolate evenly into 8 squares and place a piece on top of each indentation, then spoon the remaining cake mixture on top.

★ Bake the cupcakes in the preheated oven for 20 minutes, or until well risen and springy to the touch. Leave the cupcakes for 2–3 minutes before serving warm, dusted with sifted icing sugar.

These pretty little cupcakes are perfect for serving with coffee after dinner. Alternatively, packed into an attractive box, they make a lovely home-made gift. You will find mini paper cases in specialized cake decoration shops.

tiny chocolate cupcakes with ganache frosting

Makes 20 cupcakes

55 g/2 oz butter, softened

55 g/2 oz caster sugar

I large egg, lightly beaten

55 g/2 oz self-raising white flour

2 tbsp cocoa powder

I tbsp milk

20 chocolate-coated coffee beans, to decorate (optional)

Frosting

100 g/3½ oz plain chocolate

100 ml/3½ fl oz double cream

★ Preheat the oven to 190°C/375°F/Gas Mark 5. Put 20 double-layer mini paper cases on 2 baking trays.

★ Put the butter and sugar in a bowl and beat together until light and fluffy. Gradually beat in the egg. Sift in the flour and cocoa powder and then, using a metal spoon, fold them into the mixture. Stir in the milk.

★ Fill a piping bag, fitted with a large plain nozzle, with the mixture and pipe it into the paper cases, filling each one until half full.

★ Bake the cakes in the preheated oven for 10–15 minutes, or until well risen and firm to the touch. Transfer to a wire rack to cool.

★ To make the frosting, break the chocolate into a saucepan and add the cream. Heat gently, stirring all the time, until the chocolate has melted. Pour into a large heatproof bowl and, using an electric hand whisk, beat the mixture for 10 minutes, or until thick, glossy and cool.

★ Fill a piping bag, fitted with a large star nozzle, with the frosting and pipe a swirl on top of each cupcake. Alternatively, spoon the frosting over the top of each cupcake. Chill in the refrigerator for I hour before serving. Serve decorated with a chocolate-coated coffee bean, if liked.

The first recorded recipe for Devil's Food Chocolate Cake is from 1905 and its name is thought to have come from the fact that it is so rich and indulgent that it must be wicked and evil. Miniature versions of this classic American cake make them even more irresistible.

devil's food cakes with chocolate frosting

Makes 18 cupcakes

50 g/1³/4 oz soft tub margarine

115 g/4 oz soft dark brown sugar

2 large eggs

115 g/4 oz plain white flour

¹/2 tsp bicarbonate of soda

25 g/1 oz cocoa powder

125 ml/4 fl oz soured cream

Frosting

125 g/4¹/2 oz plain chocolate

2 tbsp caster sugar

150 ml/5 fl oz soured cream

Chocolate curls (optional)

100 g/3¹/2 oz plain chocolate

★ Preheat the oven to 180°C/350°F/Gas Mark 4. Put 18 paper baking cases in a bun tray, or put 18 double-layer paper cases on a baking tray.

★ Put the margarine, sugar, eggs, flour, bicarbonate of soda and cocoa powder in a large bowl and, using an electric hand whisk, beat together until just smooth. Using a metal spoon, fold in the soured cream. Spoon the mixture into the paper cases.

★ Bake the cupcakes in the preheated oven for 20 minutes, or until well risen and firm to the touch. Transfer to a wire rack to cool.

★ To make the frosting, break the chocolate into a heatproof bowl. Set the bowl over a saucepan of gently simmering water and heat until melted, stirring occasionally. Remove from the heat and allow to cool slightly, then whisk in the sugar and soured cream until combined. Spread the frosting over the tops of the cupcakes and leave to set in the refrigerator before serving. If liked, serve decorated with chocolate curls made by shaving plain chocolate chocolate with a potato peeler.

These cupcakes look like little cups of cappuccino coffee and are perfect for serving with mid-morning coffee.

mocha cupcakes with whipped cream

Makes 20 cupcakes

2 tbsp instant espresso coffee powder

85 g/3 oz butter

85 g/3 oz caster sugar

1 tbsp clear honey

200 ml/7 fl oz water

225 g/8 oz plain white flour

2 tbsp cocoa powder

1 tsp bicarbonate of soda

3 tbsp milk

1 large egg, lightly beaten

Topping

225 ml/8 fl oz whipping cream

cocoa powder, sifted, for dusting

★ Preheat the oven to 180°C/350°F/Gas Mark 4. Put 20 paper baking cases in 2 bun trays, or put 20 double-layer paper cases on 2 baking trays.

★ Put the coffee powder, butter, sugar, honey and water in a saucepan and heat gently, stirring, until the sugar has dissolved. Bring to the boil, then reduce the heat and simmer for 5 minutes. Pour into a large heatproof bowl and leave to cool.

★ When the mixture has cooled, sift in the flour and cocoa powder. Dissolve the bicarbonate of soda in the milk, then add to the mixture with the egg and beat together until smooth. Spoon the mixture into the paper cases.

★ Bake the cupcakes in the preheated oven for 15–20 minutes, or until well risen and firm to the touch. Transfer to a wire rack to cool.

★ For the topping, whisk the cream in a bowl until it holds its shape. Just before serving, spoon heaped teaspoonfuls of cream on top of each cake, then dust lightly with sifted cocoa powder. Store the cupcakes in the refrigerator until ready to serve.

festive
creations

Children will love to get their fangs stuck into these little cakes.
They will enjoy decorating them with creepy spiders too.

halloween cupcakes

Makes 12 cupcakes

115 g/4 oz soft tub margarine

115 g/4 oz caster sugar

2 eggs

115 g/4 oz self-raising white flour

Topping

200 g/7 oz orange ready-to-roll coloured fondant icing

icing sugar, for dusting

55 g/2 oz black ready-to-roll coloured fondant icing

black cake writing icing

white cake writing icing

★ Preheat the oven to 180°C/350°F/Gas Mark 4. Put 12 paper baking cases in a bun tray, or put 12 double-layer paper cases on a baking tray.

★ Put the margarine, sugar, eggs and flour in a bowl and, using an electric hand whisk, beat together until smooth. Spoon the mixture into the cases.

★ Bake the cupcakes in the preheated oven for 15–20 minutes, or until well risen, golden brown and firm to the touch. Transfer to a wire rack and leave to cool.

★ When the cupcakes are cold, knead the orange icing until pliable, then roll out on a surface lightly dusted with icing sugar. Using the palm of your hand, lightly rub icing sugar into the icing to prevent it from spotting. Using a 5.5-cm/2¼-inch plain round cutter, cut out 12 circles, re-rolling the icing as necessary. Place a circle on top of each cupcake.

★ Roll out the black icing on a surface lightly dusted with icing sugar. Using the palm of your hand, lightly rub icing sugar into the icing to prevent it from spotting. Using a 3-cm/1¼-inch plain round cutter, cut out 12 circles and place them on the centre of the cupcakes. Using black writing icing, pipe 8 legs on to each spider and using white writing icing, draw 2 eyes and a mouth.

February 14th was probably chosen as Valentine's Day because it was the ancient belief that birds, particularly lovebirds, began to mate on that date. Make a batch of these delicious cupcakes for the one you love. Alternatively, impress your family and friends with them.

valentine heart cupcakes

Makes 6 cupcakes

85 g/3 oz butter, softened, or soft tub margarine

85 g/3 oz caster sugar

½ tsp vanilla extract

2 eggs, lightly beaten

70 g/2½ oz plain white flour

1 tbsp cocoa powder

1 tsp baking powder

Marzipan hearts

35 g/1¼ oz marzipan

red food colouring (liquid or paste)

icing sugar, for dusting

Topping

55 g/2 oz butter, softened

115 g/4 oz icing sugar

25 g/1 oz plain chocolate, melted

6 chocolate flower decorations

★ To make the hearts, knead the marzipan until pliable, then add a few drops of red colouring and knead until evenly coloured. Roll out the marzipan to a thickness of 5 mm/¼ inch on a surface dusted with icing sugar. Using a small heart-shaped cutter, cut out 6 hearts. Place these on a tray, lined with greaseproof paper and dusted with icing sugar, and leave to dry for 3–4 hours.

★ To make the cupcakes, preheat the oven to 180°C/350°F/Gas Mark 4. Put 6 paper muffin cases in a muffin tin.

★ Put the butter, sugar and vanilla extract in a bowl and beat together until light and fluffy. Gradually add the eggs, beating well after each addition. Sift in the flour, cocoa powder and baking powder and, using a large metal spoon, fold into the mixture. Spoon the mixture into the paper cases.

★ Bake the cupcakes in the preheated oven for 20–25 minutes, or until well risen and firm to the touch. Transfer to a wire rack and leave to cool.

★ To make the topping, put the butter in a large bowl and beat until fluffy. Sift in the icing sugar and beat together until smooth. Add the melted chocolate and beat together until well mixed. When the cupcakes are cold, spread the icing on top of each cupcake and decorate with a chocolate flower.

These cupcakes are baked in muffin cases so that they are larger than the usual cupcakes. Once decorated, they look like miniature Christmas cakes. The addition of ground almonds gives a firm texture and adds a richness suitable for the occasion.

christmas cupcakes

Makes 16 cupcakes

125 g/4½ oz butter, softened

200 g/7 oz caster sugar

4–6 drops almond extract

4 eggs, lightly beaten

150 g/5½ oz self-raising white flour

175 g/6 oz ground almonds

Topping

450 g/1 lb white ready-to-roll
  fondant icing

55 g/2 oz green ready-to-roll
  coloured fondant icing

25 g/1 oz red ready-to-roll coloured
  fondant icing

icing sugar, for dusting

★ Preheat the oven to 180°C/350°F/Gas Mark 4. Put 16 paper muffin cases in a muffin tin.

★ Put the butter, sugar and almond extract in a bowl and beat together until light and fluffy. Gradually add the eggs, beating well after each addition. Add the flour and, using a large metal spoon, fold it into the mixture, then fold in the ground almonds. Spoon the mixture into the paper cases to half-fill them.

★ Bake the cakes in the preheated oven for 20 minutes, or until well risen, golden brown and firm to the touch. Transfer to a wire rack and leave to cool.

★ When the cakes are cold, knead the white icing until pliable, then roll out on a surface lightly dusted with icing sugar. Using a 7-cm/2¾-inch plain round cutter, cut out 16 circles, re-rolling the icing as necessary. Place a circle on top of each cupcake.

★ Roll out the green icing on a surface lightly dusted with icing sugar. Using the palm of your hand, rub icing sugar into the icing to prevent it from spotting. Using a holly leaf-shaped cutter, cut out 32 leaves, re-rolling the icing as necessary. Brush each leaf with a little cooled boiled water and place 2 leaves on top of each cupcake. Roll the red icing between the palms of your hands to form 48 berries and place in the centre of the leaves, to decorate.

Fairy cakes are basic cupcakes with a simple plain base and a pretty iced top. They have no connection with fairies, but were probably given their name because they are light and delicate, just like those tiny beings. Why not have a children's fairy cake birthday party?

birthday party fairy cakes

Makes 24 cupcakes

225 g/8 oz soft tub margarine

225 g/8 oz caster sugar

4 eggs

225 g/8 oz self-raising white flour

Topping

175 g/6 oz butter, softened

350 g/12 oz icing sugar

a variety of small sweets and chocolates, sugar-coated chocolates, dried fruits, edible sugar flower shapes, cake decorating sprinkles, sugar strands, silver or gold dragées (cake decoration balls) and hundreds and thousands

various coloured tubes of writing icing

candles and candleholders (optional)

★ Preheat the oven to 180°C/350°F/Gas Mark 4. Put 24 paper baking cases in a bun tray, or put 24 double-layer paper cases on a baking tray.

★ Put the margarine, sugar, eggs and flour in a large bowl and, using an electric hand whisk, beat together until just smooth. Spoon the mixture into the paper cases.

★ Bake the cupcakes in the preheated oven for 15–20 minutes, or until well risen, golden brown and firm to the touch. Transfer to a wire rack and leave to cool.

★ To make the icing, put the butter in a bowl and beat until fluffy. Sift in the icing sugar and beat together until smooth and creamy.

★ When the cupcakes are cold, spread the icing on top of each cupcake, then decorate to your choice and, if desired, place a candle in the top of each.

Easter eggs have been part of Easter festivities for a long time. Miniature chocolate eggs, nestled on top of chocolate cupcakes, are the perfect treat for Easter holidays.

easter cupcakes

Makes 12 cupcakes

115 g/4 oz butter, softened, or soft tub margarine

115 g/4 oz caster sugar

2 eggs, lightly beaten

85 g/3 oz self-raising white flour

25 g/1 oz cocoa powder

Topping

85 g/3 oz butter, softened

175 g/6 oz icing sugar

1 tbsp milk

2–3 drops of vanilla extract

two 130-g/4¾-oz packets mini chocolate candy shell eggs

★ Preheat the oven to 180°C/350°F/Gas Mark 4. Put 12 paper baking cases in a bun tray, or put 12 double-layer paper cases on a baking tray.

★ Put the butter and sugar in a bowl and beat together until light and fluffy. Gradually add the eggs, beating well after each addition. Sift in the flour and cocoa powder and, using a large metal spoon, fold into the mixture. Spoon the mixture into the paper cases.

★ Bake the cupcakes in the preheated oven for 15–20 minutes, or until well risen and firm to the touch. Transfer to a wire rack and leave to cool.

★ To make the butter cream topping, put the butter in a bowl and beat until fluffy. Sift in the icing sugar and beat together until well mixed, adding the milk and vanilla extract.

★ When the cupcakes are cold, put the icing in a piping bag, fitted with a large star nozzle, and pipe a circle around the edge of each cupcake to form a nest. Place chocolate eggs in the centre of each nest, to decorate.

It doesn't need to be a golden or silver anniversary to serve these beautiful cupcakes. Any anniversary or festive celebration will do. Look for silver or gold foil cake cases in cake decoration shops.

gold & silver anniversary cupcakes

Makes 24 cupcakes

225 g/8 oz butter, softened

225 g/8 oz caster sugar

1 tsp vanilla extract

4 large eggs, lightly beaten

225 g/8 oz self-raising white flour

5 tbsp milk

Topping

175 g/6 oz unsalted butter

350 g/12 oz icing sugar

25 g/1 oz silver or gold dragées
  (cake decoration balls)

★ Preheat the oven to 180°C/350°F/Gas Mark 4. Put 24 silver or gold foil cake cases in bun trays, or arrange them on baking trays.

★ Put the butter, sugar and vanilla extract in a bowl and beat together until light and fluffy. Gradually add the eggs, beating well after each addition. Add the flour and, using a large metal spoon, fold into the mixture with the milk. Spoon the mixture into the paper cases.

★ Bake the cupcakes in the preheated oven for 15–20 minutes, or until well risen and firm to the touch. Transfer to a wire rack and leave to cool.

★ To make the topping, put the butter in a large bowl and beat until fluffy. Sift in the icing sugar and beat together until well mixed. Put the topping in a piping bag, fitted with a medium star-shaped nozzle.

★ When the cupcakes are cold, pipe circles of icing on top of each cupcake to cover the tops. Sprinkle over the silver or gold dragées before serving.

Baby shower parties allow your family and friends to share the joy and excitement of welcoming a new life into the world. To ice these cupcakes, you could choose pink for a girl or blue for a boy.

baby shower cupcakes with sugared almonds

Makes 24 cupcakes

400 g/14 oz butter, softened

400 g/14 oz caster sugar

finely grated rind of 2 lemons

8 eggs, lightly beaten

400 g/14 oz self-raising white flour

Topping

350 g/12 oz icing sugar

red or blue food colouring (liquid or paste)

24 sugared almonds

★ Preheat the oven to 180°C/350°F/Gas Mark 4. Put 24 paper muffin cases in a muffin tin.

★ Put the butter, sugar and lemon rind in a bowl and beat together until light and fluffy. Gradually add the eggs, beating well after each addition. Add the flour and, using a large metal spoon, fold into the mixture. Spoon the mixture into the paper cases to half-fill them.

★ Bake the cupcakes in the preheated oven for 20–25 minutes, or until well risen, golden brown and firm to the touch. Transfer to a wire rack and leave to cool.

★ When the cakes are cold, make the topping. Sift the icing sugar into a bowl. Add 6–8 teaspoons of hot water and stir until the mixture is smooth and thick enough to coat the back of a wooden spoon. Dip a skewer into the red or blue food colouring, then stir it into the icing until it is evenly coloured pink or pale blue.

★ Spoon the icing on top of each cupcake. Top each with a sugared almond and leave to set for about 30 minutes, before serving.

This stunning centrepiece is a festive cake with a difference, since each guest has his or her own individual cupcake. If you are inviting more than 48 guests, just increase the number of cupcakes you make.

the cupcake wedding cake

Makes 48 cupcakes

450 g/1 lb butter, softened

450 g/1 lb caster sugar

2 tsp vanilla extract

8 large eggs, lightly beaten

450 g/1 lb self-raising white flour

150 ml/5 fl oz milk

Topping

550 g/1 lb 4 oz icing sugar

48 ready-made sugar roses, or 48 small fresh rose buds gently rinsed and left to dry on kitchen paper

To assemble the cake

one 50-cm/20-inch, one 40-cm/16-inch, one 30-cm/12-inch and one 20-cm/8-inch sandblasted glass disc with polished edges, or silver cake boards

13 white or Perspex cake pillars

1 small bouquet of fresh flowers in a small vase

★ Preheat the oven to 180°C/350°F/Gas Mark 4. Put 48 paper baking cases in a bun tray, or put 48 double-layer paper cases on a baking tray.

★ Put the butter, sugar and vanilla extract in a bowl and beat together until light and fluffy. Gradually add the eggs, beating well after each addition. Add the flour and, using a large metal spoon, fold into the mixture with the milk. Spoon the mixture into the paper cases.

★ Bake the cupcakes in the preheated oven for 15–20 minutes, or until well risen and firm to the touch. Transfer to a wire rack and leave to cool.

★ To make the topping, sift the icing sugar into a large bowl. Add 3–4 tablespoons hot water and stir until the mixture is smooth and thick enough to coat the back of a wooden spoon. Spoon the icing on top of each cupcake. Store the cupcakes in an airtight container for up to one day.

★ On the day of serving, carefully place the sugar roses or rose buds on top of each cupcake. To arrange the cupcakes, place the largest disc or board on a table where the finished display is to be. Stand 5 pillars on the disc and arrange some of the cupcakes on the base. Continue with the remaining bases, pillars (using only 4 pillars to support each remaining tier) and cupcakes to make 4 tiers, standing the bouquet of flowers in the centre of the top tier.

index